WAS IT SOMETHING I SAID?

A Guide to Coaching Female Athletes

Vanessa Sullivan
and
Mike Tully

1st Edition, Vanessa Sullivan and Mike Tully
Published by The Center for Sport Success
Bloomfield, NJ.
Publishing date: Feb. 2015

WAS IT SOMETHING I SAID?
A Guide to Coaching Female Athletes

Vanessa Sullivan and Mike Tully

A publication of
THE CENTER FOR SPORT SUCCESS
900 Valley Road.
Suite D-1
Clifton, NJ 07013
(973) 800-5836

Library of Congress
Catalogue Card Number

ISBN:-9781505914870

Edited by Kirk Nicewonger
Cover design by Vanessa Sullivan

DEDICATIONS

To my family and friends for their constant support. To Maria Elena Bellinger and Ed Saggio, can't say thank you enough. I'm where I am and who I am because of you! To anyone who feels misunderstood, this one's for you.
— Vanessa Sullivan

To my wife, Patty, my teammate for life. To mom and dad. To Patty Sullivan, who gave me a chance to coach. To my co-author Vanessa Sullivan, who has made me a better coach.
— Mike Tully

Table of Contents

Chapter 1

He Thinks I'm Fat

Let's begin by teaching some young athletes how to shoot a free throw:

Coach says to boy: Be balanced, keep your eyes on the back of the rim, and spread your fingers on the ball.

Boy thinks: He doesn't know what he's talking about. I'll do it my way.

Coach says to girl: Be balanced, keep your eyes on the back of the rim, and spread your fingers on the ball.

Girl thinks: He thinks I'm fat.

Chapter 2

More Than Just Physical

Vanessa:

I don't think people truly understand what it's like to coach teenage girls. And I'm not saying that boys don't have any issues or drama. They do. There's just such a sensitivity that comes with females. Let's face it, men don't understand women. There's even a book titled, "Everything Men Know About Women." It's 120 blank pages.

Sometimes I think male coaches have read and reread that book. They just don't get it about girls. I have learned that everything in life comes down to how you perceive the situation: mentally and emotionally. And, as Chapter 1 shows, girls perceive things differently.

Sports are incredibly mental. There is the pressure to perform well, and the importance in handling the heckling and even the cheering of the crowds. Then there are the constant demands of the clock, the next shot, or the crucial game point serve. Throw in teammate issues, communication breakdowns, the game plan and, finally, misunderstandings between the player and coach, and you've got a lot going on! Outside the gym, there's even more: family, finances, school.

Again, boys go through hardships, too, but girls perceive and process these issues differently, as we will see.

By no means do I mean to stereotype. Every human being is unique. That's what makes us all so fascinating! Sometimes WE don't even understand *ourselves*, let alone our whole gender. I don't want anyone to read these stories and examples and think, "that's not me" and shut down and close the book. It might not be you, today. It might not be you, next year. It might not ever be you!

At the same time, some females might connect to these stories. They might even think I'm writing this story about them. That is what is important about all of this: Understanding multiple people could receive the same feedback and perceive it several different ways.

For now, let's just say sports are more than just physical activities, and if you're smart you'll coach that way.

Tip: When you coach girls, there's a lot going on.

Chapter 3

How the Passion Dies

Vanessa:

My four-year career in college volleyball was not a particularly good experience. Unfortunately the mental, emotional, and fundamental aspects of building a team were not addressed. The only time we really bonded was outside of the gym, or when we were all trying to keep it together and not quit the sport we loved. A lot of us had motivation all right. Our motivation was to make it through four years of college volleyball.

When the passion starts fading, frankly I believe no amount of talent alone can create a winning team. If none of the girls want to be there and play hard and compete, you cannot produce a true championship team.

Over those four years, I had reached the weakest point I've ever been in my life, mentally. I cried more tears in those four years than could fill my Inground pool at home. I never felt supported, appreciated or valued. I was even told I was the worst recruit my coach ever had, and she wished she had the girl from the other team we were playing because that girl was so much better than I was. In the middle of a time out. In front of everyone. When the score was 23-23 and we still could have won the game. In that exact moment I emotionally went to a place where I thought I would never return. I had completely fallen out of love with this sport.

I finished school breaking three different records, and was a four-time academic honor roll student. Twice in my career I was named Libero of the Week in our conference.

You might think she was pushing me because she truly believed I could do great things. I can assure you that was not her intention. I spoke out of turn in the time out and all the anger and frustrated emotions went directly toward me. That's as simple as it was. But it was too much to constantly endure over four years.

Not until I started playing at open gyms when I moved back home did I find that passion again. The people I played with, and the owners of the facility we played in constantly gave me praise and feedback. They truly brought me back to life.

The one thing I learned was what I DIDN'T want to become when I decided to coach. I love being aggressive, I love pushing my teams. Scaring them a little bit by giving consequences for not reaching goals during drills is something I think is important. I consider myself a tough coach, just like my high school coach was. Just like her, I love it when I ask you to work on something and as a player you listen and commit to working on it. When you correct what I ask you to, and you give me 100% of your hustle and commitment, I don't care how the score ends. I'm proud. And if I'm proud, my team will be the first to know it. And I don't wait until the end of the season to let them know. They make an impressive play, I'll be the first one jumping up and down in excitement. Because I've been there. I've played in both situations. And I know which coach got me fired up to work harder and harder, and which one pushed me shut down mentally.

Mike:

Coaches should keep in mind this great management principle: Catch someone doing something right. It will make them feel good. Author and coaching guru Ken Blanchard said, "People who feel good about themselves produce good results, and people who produce good results feel good about themselves."

One year a coaching colleague approached me with tip about my own team. He had heard (maybe because the girls told him, knowing that it would get back to me) that girls were beginning to think that nothing they did could ever please me. They were starting to believe they couldn't do anything right. Immediately I looked closely at what I was saying. I changed it and the results were quick and magical.

That's an important lesson. Always have someone on your staff who can give you honest feedback about the way you're coming across.

Tip: If your players do something right, tell them right then! Don't wait until the end of the season.

Chapter 4

Why Was She Crying?

From Mike:

Call it the danger zone. It's the 15 minutes after every game when the coach talks to the team about what just happened.

There are two things you must know about the post-game talk. One, the words must be chosen carefully because they will shape everything going forward. Words can build up or break down. Two, these words must be chosen at exactly the time when emotions are running high.

It's a delicate, explosive mix, a real test for a coach. And I remember one of the nights I failed it badly.

Our college volleyball team had just lost. That happened a lot, and the frustration was building. One thing about the game really bothered me, and I wanted to let my players know it.

Looking out at the 12 women in front of me, I launched into a rant, with particular attention to body language. "You can't complain about playing time and then slouch on the bench," I said. "When I need to put in a substitute and look down the bench and see you daydreaming or slumped back in your seat, I'm not going to put you in. Sit up in your seat, lean forward toward the game, and look like you care."

It seemed logical to me. This wasn't kindergarten, after all. It was the NCAA! If anything, in my mind I deserved points for gallantry because I had taken pains not call out anyone by name. I had one player in mind but didn't look at her directly. Instead I just ran my eyes over the whole team, hoping they would get the message.

It was a *disaster*.

The girl I had in mind never reacted. That was the bad news. There was even worse news: Another girl, a model citizen with whom I had no complaint, burst into tears.

Those tears made a big impression on me, but not the one they should have. Over the years I've brought it up when coaches swap stories on the perils of coaching. Unfortunately, it never occurred to me that I was missing something basic and profound about coaching women.

Men and women look at things in fundamentally different ways. You can't be an effective coach unless you understand that. Back then there was so much I didn't know about coaching females. Regrettably, I didn't even know that I didn't know.

Now, 15 years later, there's still a ton I don't know about coaching females. The positive note is I, at least now, know there's so much I don't know. That's why I'm so happy to have Vanessa Sullivan as a writing partner. She's a female athlete with stories to tell; stories that can help all coaches - male and female - do a better job of leading female athletes.

When Vanessa and I first started meeting to put together this book, she sounded as if she had been a fly on the wall hearing every word I've ever said at a practice, in a huddle, and in a post-game talk. Each story she told made me grimace, smack my head and say, "Yup, I've done that." It was like she was reciting my coaching history. And it wasn't pretty.

For instance, when Vanessa heard about the girl who burst into tears, she instantly came up with a thought that had never occurred to me. "Maybe she cried because she was the one who was on the edge of her seat ready to go in, but you never looked at her. You kept looking at the girl who was slouching."

Vanessa, where were you 15 years ago?

Well, 15 years ago Vanessa was an athlete working hard for award-winning success and living through experiences that can now help coaches. Vanessa has already made me a better coach. If you coach females, she can do the same for you.

Tip: Know that you don't know.

Chapter 5

What Girls Want in a Talk

From Vanessa:

This subject is a tough one because there are so many different scenarios.

> *We just won. We just lost. We just tied. We had a game-changing or season-changing injury. The referees blew the game for us. We won a championship. We lost a championship.*

There are a hundred different ways a game can end, and each result requires a different speech.

But here's what I will say. Every single game stirs up some kind of emotion. Whether they're positive or negative, emotions are flying high, and if you are a coach it is critical to recognize this. If your team lost, the players know they played worse than the other team, and they typically are just as disappointed as you are. Sometimes more, if one girl feels she let down the team. It is your job and responsibility as a coach to recognize this early, and not kick them while they're down. Kicking them when they're down will hurt the next day's practice indefinitely. And what happens if the team loses another game, or three or four games in a row? Now your athletes will dread every game, and every practice will be worse than the one before. I promise the momentum of the season will quickly shift from motivated to dreaded.

My best advice is to recognize your own team's effort, and to focus on what the other team did right. This is really important! The other team won, so they had more positives: better statistics, faster offense, stronger defense, and/or more communication, etc. You always want to focus on the positives, whether it is your team or not. That is a tricky concept to grasp.

The most obvious example is a soccer game going to a shootout. Sarah has to score the goal, otherwise her team loses. She misses the kick and the game is over. When the team huddles up and you talk about the game, as a whole, it would be best to leave out the obvious statement of "If Sarah would've made that shot ..." It's not necessary, and it's not beneficial. We all were at the game; we saw what happened. Sarah knows she missed that shot, so telling her isn't any news to her. Don't even bring it up.

I'm not kidding, don't bring it up.

There is never a moment in team sports where one person lost the whole game for everyone. Build your remarks around the team. It is detrimental if you don't. If you coach an individual sport, like tennis, your athlete is well aware she hit the last ball into the net. It is best to comment on positives, even if they're for the other team. Think of it as reverse feedback.

Let's say you're coaching softball, and your players are not hitting well. After the game you can say something along the lines of, "She's a good pitcher and she had a good day today. She did a really good job of placing the ball where she wanted to. Her change of speeds kept us off balance. And that's what this game came down to. We'll tip our cap to her and get her the next time." Keep things positive and blame-free.

Given a choice between telling your team "They out-hustled us" or "We didn't hustle," go with the first one! It's a subtle difference, but at least you're acknowledging that your team hustled and tried. With the second one, you're choosing a negative. It's quite possible that your athletes were trying, and very hard, but the other team was just that much better.

Just as important is following up the tone of a good post-game talk with a positive tone to open the next practice. It's crucial! Everyone has gone home and slept on it. The next day at practice you can talk a little bit more specifically about various aspects of the game. In breaking down the softball game, for instance, you might expand on the theme of the opposing pitcher's location and change of speeds. "We let a lot of good pitches go by, and once that pitcher gets ahead early in the count, she's even tougher. Today we're going to work on being more aggressive."

Simple as that. I don't dwell on it, I don't bring up specific players, and giving a number goes further than just stating my opinion. Facts trump opinions from coaches, sorry, but they do. If I say, "Girls, we didn't hit well last night," they think I'm being mean. If I say, "Girls, we fell behind in the count in 75 percent of our at-bats yesterday," the athletes don't have to worry about specific blame. They can just agree, "Wow, we really didn't hit well…"

Tip: Find a positive.

Chapter 6

Disaster on the Delaware

From Mike:

My misadventures with the female psyche go back much further than that night of tears in the gym. One summer day our family decided to go white-water rafting on the Delaware River. My wife and I took our three daughters and a summer guest and headed to our adventure. What paradise! Out there, far from land and phones, I dove into the water, climbed back on the raft, and dove in again. Just imagine a dolphin frolicking around a cruise ship. On that day, the world was my playground, and the only worry was our supply of sunscreen.

Actually, that turned out to be not quite true. There was a bigger problem than sunscreen, though I didn't realize it until too late. To say that my wife didn't enjoy our excursion would be an understatement. She was furious at my diving and all-around activity. This baffled me. We were out for fun, right? So what was wrong with playing?

Not long after, still baffled, I saw a stray book in the office. It was about relationships, and the challenge of living with the person you love. Too bad the book hadn't shown up before our ill-fated river ride. In the first few pages, it captured everything that had gone wrong. Men and women not only ARE different, they VALUE different things. Men value independence. That's why sitting in the middle of the river was so much fun. Anyone who wanted to bother me would have had to swim out to do so.

Women on the other hand, value cooperation and shared experiences. For my wife, staying in the raft and rowing together not only would have been more efficient, it would have been more FUN. What I thought was an innocent dive overboard was, to my wife, a lack of cooperation.

I can't remember if she showed her irritation during the trip or after. Or both. If she was sending out signals, I missed them.

Figures.

Tip: Girls value shared effort.

Chapter 7

Abandon Ship!

From Vanessa:

You want to talk about quitting on your team? I used to play for a coach (female) who ran out the door every time we lost. Players would have to put all the equipment away and leave without any feedback from her. She was so mad at us that no words were exchanged. I hope this doesn't come as news to too many coaches, either male or female, but abandoning your players when they need some leadership is not productive.

Later on I coached with a person who would go to the opposite extreme. He laughed off losses in hopes of keeping things light. That doesn't work, either. Being too passive about a loss is just as bad as being too aggressive. Your players want to know you CARE, and they also want to be SUPPORTED.

Finding that happy medium is hard to do, and it comes with a lot of practice. Through a lot of trial and error I've found the most effective way to talk to your team after a game is to focus on how the other team was successful, talk about the effort your team put forth, give the team an opportunity to express their opinions and frustrations so you can all build and grow as a team, and then go home and get a good night's rest. Tomorrow is a new day to create your practice plan, and everyone will come in with a fresher mindset.

How many times have you heard of a person quitting because their coach gave them so much grief they lost interest and passion for the sport? Poor coaching ranks among the top reasons why girls quit organized sports teams. According to a post by author Brooke DeLenche on the blog momsTeam, "Of the 11 reasons cited by girls in a classic 1988 study as to why they dropped out of sports, the fourth-highest was that the coach was a poor teacher; number nine was that the coach played favorites. Coaches who berate and belittle girls turn sports into such a hurtful, harmful experience that dropping out becomes for many a way to avoid further damage to their self-esteem."

Coaches who don't support girls will lose them. Everyone needs support in his or her own way. Some people can't handle the pressure of sports and performing. Others want more playing time, but that isn't realistic considering their skill level.

Whatever the situation may be, I've found great coaches simply want the best for their athletes. They don't want to hurt them, cause them pain, or make them forget why they started playing the game in the first place.

DeLenche's momsTeam post says, "Girls continue to drop out of sports at six times the rate of boys."

Soccer legend Mia Hamm is a notable example of someone who hung in there, no matter what the challenge or the difficulty. At one time, she held the record for most international goals. She's been quoted saying, "I am a member of a team, and I rely on the team, I defer to it and sacrifice for it, because the team, not the individual, is the ultimate champion."

But Mia Hamms don't come along every day.

What if we found some ways to cut the number of athletes who abandon ship? What if we found some ways to keep the relationship strong between coaches and players, even for the girls who are never seeing playing time? This book's goal is to do just that. It's to help you as a coach understand the pressures, struggles, and needs of your female athletes.

Mike:

While finishing up this book, I came across an online article on best bosses and worst bosses. That makes sense. You would remember the best. And for sure you'd recall the worst.

Coaching is the same. There are the best and there are the worst. I've been both. Many of my former athletes keep in touch on social media. Twice I've been invited to a former player's wedding. One athlete, tragically deceased, had this sentence in his obituary: John loved volleyball.

Too often, though, there are players who ran out of the gym crying, and who would be perfectly happy never to see or hear from me again.

Care for your players. Wins and championships are nice. They're great, actually. But nothing matches the feeling that comes when a former player tells you that you made a difference.

Tip: Coaches who don't support girls will lose them.

Chapter 8

How to Tear Down a Player

From Mike:

Tom Hanks, playing manager Jimmy Dugan in the movie "A League of Their Own," famously tells one of his players, "There's no crying in baseball."

This line, delivered to Evelyn, played by Bitty Schram, ranks as the 54th-best quote in the history of American cinema, according to the American Film Institute.

No wonder. It captures the confusion and frustration of males when confronted with female tears. A closer look at the scene, however, should take some of the confusion out of the situation. Evelyn cries because the manager blames the loss on her. "You let the tying run get to second, and we lost the lead because of you. You start using your head. That's the lump that's three feet above your ass."

Beautiful. He singles out a player, blames her for the loss, and then belittles her intelligence, mixing in some salty language. It's the grand slam of bad coaching. All he leaves out is some reference to her weight. Doris (Rosie O'Donnell) tries to intervene, saying, "Why don't you leave her alone, Jimmy?" He waves aside her objection, returning to his point. "There's no crying in baseball."

In case you're thinking my athletes have been a parade of whimpering emotional wrecks, that's not the case at all. Most of my athletes have been incredibly strong individuals who are living lives of quality and distinction. My point is that there have been times when girls on my team have cried. Sometimes I've understood why, other times not. More than anything, tears symbolize the emotional gulf between male and female.

Writing this book with Vanessa can give me a blueprint to grow. Even Jimmy Dugan grew. Later in the movie, there's a wonderful scene where you can see him struggling to control his frustration as he explains a situation to a player. He literally shakes with the effort. He still doesn't understand exactly what's going on, but he knows that SOMETHING is going on.

That's where a lot of us are in coaching girls.

Tip: Control your frustration.

Chapter 9

What Game Are You Watching?

From Vanessa:

So many times males ask me, "Why is she crying?" I am baffled that the question even comes up. It makes me wonder what game these coaches are watching. I pick up on what's going on with the girls: body language, comments under their breath, and the eye-rolling.

When girls walk away from a team high-five, or when one of them cops an attitude- I notice all of it. I've been in those shoes. I've been a college volleyball player. I've been a club volleyball player. I can relate. Being on a team with 15 girls, I know what to look for and I know how it affects teams. I've seen it. I've lived it.

What baffles me in relation to sports and gender is that, in my experience, males view sports as very black or white. Females see everything EXCEPT black and white. They see the full spectrum: emotions, insecurities, pressure-handling. Not that these topics don't apply to guys as well. It's just that these topics affect us differently. As females we take everything personally, whether it is or not. We just do.

For instance, I was being recruited for college volleyball and the coach came to one of my games to see me play. Afterward, he told me, "It's nothing personal, but we already have this position filled. Frankly, we just don't need you." He directly told me it wasn't personal, but I walked away taking it 100 percent personally. As a female I'm wondering, "What could I have done differently for him to give me a different answer?"

In the TV series, "Columbo," the great detective tells a suspect, "It's nothing personal." She replies, "When someone tells you it's not personal, that's when it's about to get VERY personal."

Yes, the suspect was a she.

Tip: Girls take it personally.

Chapter 10

Your Tone Says It All

From Mike:

Nonverbal World, a blog on behavior, explains why women are experts at nonverbal communication. "Women give birth to children and face a great challenge of understanding every condition that babies are going through only by observing their facial expressions, gestures, postures, movements and voice ..."

All these behaviors -- facial expressions, gestures, etc. -- are on display everywhere in a girl's universe: at practice, in games and even in the school hallways. It's not just that girls pick up on these cues. It's that they have no choice. Absorbing nonverbal information is in their DNA. They can't flip a switch and turn it off.

Dave Cross, a coach specializing in mental training, preaches that only 7 percent of a statement's meaning comes from the words. Tone, facial expression, body language and other factors make up the rest.

When you combine what Cross says with what we know about females and non-verbal communication, it's no wonder that the post-game talk, as well as any communication between player and athlete, is a danger zone.

Back in my sports writing days, my boss, baseball Hall of Fame columnist Milton Richman, once said, "You can study baseball as much as you want. You can interview players. You can attend hundreds of games. There is no way you can ever understand what it's like to play professionally unless you've done it."

Richman knew what he was talking about because, unlike many other sportswriters, he had played professionally. He knew what it was like to play in front of a critical audience. He knew about internal politics, the jealousies, cliques. He knew who took the game seriously and who didn't. He knew which teammates he could trust in a crucial situation. And which ones he couldn't.

One step forward in my growth as a coach came when I began to realize there is a different world going on within the team. It's a world that can't be measured by statistics or by spectacular plays.

Vanessa, however, could probably pick out some things on film. That gives me an idea. I'd like to video a game then watch it with her, inviting her to look for signs of good chemistry. And, of course, bad chemistry.

You don't need film, however, to understand the concept of different worlds. Just take your dog for a walk. You're lost in your thoughts, pretty much oblivious to your surroundings. Dogs are different. They know about the cat under the car, the raccoon in the bushes, and, of course, the territorial markings left by other dogs. And they sure don't care about your work schedule tomorrow.

Whatever example you use, the coach on the sideline and the females on the field operate in different worlds. On the bench, I'm recording the black and white of data: What's the score? Who got the points? Meanwhile, in the game, the athletes are trying to process hundreds of nonverbal signals.

A lot of those signals come from the bench. Players tend to look to the coach after every play. You better make sure what they're seeing is positive. This took me a long time to learn. One of my college players complained that I would drop my head into my hands whenever she made a mistake. She was right. Who knows how many points that habit cost our team?

Now I work hard on my style during games. I do not make eye contact with players. I keep specialized notes instead. My female coaching colleagues handle the contact with the players. This works so much better for our team. I wish I could say that I was better at handling my emotions during a game. But to avoid sending the wrong nonverbal cues to my athletes, I let other coaches do what they do best and I do something I hope is more constructive. Every once in a while I will revert and say something or let my body language slip. That's when one of my co-coaches must remind me that my tone or actions were not helpful.

Tip: Watch your body language and tone!

Chapter 11

The Secret World of Girls

Vanessa:

Cathy was one of the best players on a team I was coaching. She was quiet and very quirky. With just one conversation, you could see how fragile she was. She had a nervous laugh, and her hands were always jittery. Her sentences were filled with "umms" and "ohs" after every word. A typical conversation would go like this:

"Cathy, what happened on that play?"

"Oh, no! Umm, the ball was like, oh, it was OK. I just, I don't know -- I, umm, swung, no, umm, elbow was bent, so, oh, you know, like it was just really bad."

I would blank stare at her, back away slowly, and try my best to be positive.

"All right guys, next play!"

It was after a practice when my assistant came to me about Cathy. She sounded concerned. We dismissed the girls and the story came out.

"I just walked into the locker room and saw Cathy standing in front of the mirror measuring her waist with her hands."

I wish I could say this hit me like a truck. It shouldn't be a shock that girls have issues with their bodies. With a team of teenage girls, what exactly did I expect? That everyone and everything was going to be perfect?

Immediately I thought, "Now what? Now what do I do?" First we had to tell our club director. Part of me was thinking, "Thank God I'm handling this the right way." Another part of me was feeling like I was about to rat out a vulnerable person and watch their whole life come crashing down. But we had to tell the boss.

Next came telling the parents, something that I was nervous about doing. All I wanted to do was coach. But that's not realistic. A coach is so much more than a teacher. A coach should be a mentor, a friend, a safe haven if need be. Coaches have responsibilities as adults and as human beings. I knew (or thought I knew) exactly what I was signing up for when I began to coach. But to actually have to have these conversations with parents was something else. No one signs up for that.

Cathy's father thanked us for talking to him about the issue. He actually knew about it, and told us she was seeing a therapist. I felt so much weight fall off my shoulders. I did what I was supposed to do.

Then her father thanked me again, saying how good it felt to have coaches so in tune with players that they noticed something was wrong. He meant it, and that's what hurt. His words were like a shot to the chest. I felt all the weight on my shoulders again. Truthfully, I hadn't known. I hadn't noticed at all. Had my assistant not walked in on her in the locker room, we might never have known.

Eventually the season ended, with no serious damage. But there's a message here. There are always issues percolating on a team. A lot of times with teenage girls it's an eating disorder.

Citing a 2011 study, the National Eating Disorders Association says, "By age 6, girls especially start to express concerns about their own weight or shape. Forty to sixty percent of elementary school girls (ages 6-12) are concerned about their weight or about becoming too fat. This concern endures through life."

If you don't know what's going on privately, it's very easy to get frustrated at something that's happening in the game. A girl might be making some uncharacteristic physical and/or mental errors. I remember thinking she was being lazy, but really she was famished from not eating and couldn't perform well.

If you don't know what's going on privately, you may ask yourself, "What the heck is going on with her today?" And sometimes when you find out what's really going on, you'll wish you never even asked.

Chances are that, like me, you didn't sign up for these issues. You just want to coach. It's not that easy. The issues are there. They are likely to come up, most likely when you least expect it. Don't let them blindside you like they blindsided me.

Mike:

I'm very fortunate to be coaching in a school that has an excellent training staff (one male and one female), as well as a great counseling office.

Whenever I see that a girl has lost weight or shown any other dramatic change in appearance, I feel I can go either to the trainers or to the counselor and report it.

Sometimes it turns out there is a normal reason for the change. Perhaps the athlete has been working out, gone on a (healthy) diet, or has recently been sick. It is always reassuring to know that nothing is amiss.

On occasion, however, I've heard the counselor say, "Yes, we're keeping an eye on her."

In either case, you feel good about reporting your concerns.

If you're in a situation where there is no counselor, principal, or training staff, make it your business to find someone in whom you can confide. As Vanessa says, sometimes it's the head of your traveling squad, an AAU official or even a coaching colleague.

Know this at the start of every season: When you coach girls, it's not hard to imagine that somewhere within your group there are issues about food intake. You never want to be in a situation where something bad happens and you regret not speaking up.

Tip: Girls have an early and lifelong concern about their weight.

Chapter 12

What Slows Girls Down

Mike:

A career as a sportswriter has given me a chance to talk to world champion athletes and coaches. By listening closely, you can pick up clues about success. Strangely, the most insightful tip came at the world luge championship in Lake Placid, N.Y.

Who would think that anyone crazy enough to sled down a mountain course at death-defying speeds could offer thoughtful insight to athletes everywhere? And yet here it is.

I asked the athlete, "What's the most important thing about your sport?"

He replied, "There is nothing that can make you go faster. You can only eliminate the things that slow you down."

Wow. That quote has remained with me for years, gaining more meaning over time. First it reminded me of sport psychology, where my mentor Dr. Rob Gilbert says, "At a certain point, you're not going to get any bigger, stronger or faster. But you can always change your attitude."

See? You can be a perfect 10 on the skill scale, but if you're only a 7 on the confidence scale, you will perform only at a 7. There's nothing that can make you go faster, but your mind can slow you down.

This especially applies to coaching girls. You can do a great job of teaching them how to play. Then it's important to LET them play.

As I've mentioned in earlier pages, I've learned this the hard way. It all came to a head after a loss when my fellow coaches took me aside and said that my words and actions on the sideline were hurting more than they were helping. These coaches did me a great service with their candor. We rearranged things on our team, and we've bounced back with a lot of victories.

If your team isn't playing well, maybe it isn't how fast they can go. Maybe it's about what's slowing them down.

Tip: You can hurt your team with the wrong words and actions.

Chapter 13

Why Dishonesty Kills

Vanessa:

Stating the obvious: dishonesty doesn't work. Not for boys, not for girls. But for girls it's a real killer. Girls are emotional. That mother quality is somewhere in us. We want to be loved and to love others and to feel a part of a team, a community, a family. If you tell us you need us and that what we contribute is valuable, it really helps. It keeps us sane, keeps us grounded and keeps us from overthinking, something we do too often.

If we receive false hope and lies, we will avoid the situation, change our behavior, and lose interest. We'll stop working hard at practice. We'll stop being team players and supporting the girls in the game. All of a sudden a loud, cheerful bench is quiet and hostile, with players in their own heads and whispering comments under their breath.

Of course, there's a difference between being honest and blunt. I watched a male coach say to one of his former players, "Well, be honest with yourself: Are you in the best weight shape as you were when you were playing this season?" This particular athlete had an eating disorder she was finally managing. Now here comes her coach calling attention to her weight. She cried in my arms. Meanwhile, the coach didn't understand why she was so emotional about it. When I told him, he said, "Ugh! Females! This is why I like coaching boys. We don't take things so personally!"

Sometimes I wonder if men think we *like* to overthink things and take them personally. As if we enjoy being super-sensitive.

I've seen a lot of team meetings and meetings between players and coaches. It's sad how different the two meetings are. Coaches will say to their co-workers, "She could never, ever play at this level," and three minutes later tell that same player, "If you keep working hard you'll be a great part of this team in the upcoming season. We really need you and we see you as a definite option for the lineup."

In the weeks after, the girl works her tail off and is confused when she doesn't get the same reps or playing time as others. Her coach had given her false hope. That's where the emotions come in. People quit, people feel betrayed and problems arise. Honesty is hard. But there are ways to keep it honest, and keep the player feeling excited.

Example: "Right now, the stats show that these girls should be in the starting lineup, and they are performing really well. I always notice and appreciate what you bring to practice, and although you aren't a starter I don't want you to think you are replaceable. We value your athleticism very much, and being such a strong practice player allows the other girls to perform as well as they do, because you are challenging them and helping them get better every single day. Thank you for helping this program grow. If there are any opportunities to get you some playing time this year I will absolutely do my best to do so; you really deserve it! Keep working hard."

Being an assistant coach makes me the middle "man" between the (male) head coach and the (female) athletes. A lot of players approach me. They let me know exactly what they are thinking: the good, the bad, and the inappropriate. I tell them how to proceed, what to eliminate, what to highlight, and what words to cut out if they want to be respectful. At heart, what they're trying to do is ask the coach, the main boss, "How can I do more? How do I become that person or teammate you are proud to have, and how can I change my game so you are impressed and want me on the court?" They just want to be recognized. They want to be good enough. So I empathize with them. Because whether it's sports, a job, education, love life, salary, family, body, health, makeup, or your hair -- everyone's always trying to feel good enough.

Mike:

It's never easy to tell anyone one particular truth about why they're not playing, namely, that the other person is playing better. You can say that the lineup is not permanent and that things can change. But chances are that once you say the other person is playing better, your words are no longer getting through.

One season a player told me that I was showing favoritism. I asked her to be more specific, and she mentioned a name. I replied, "You better believe I favor her. She is the best player in the county."

Trouble is, earlier in the season I had emphasized that all roles on the team were up for grabs. Everyone could compete for a job. After hearing this, the girl wanted to know why one job was not being contested.

Make sure of every word when you talk to your players. If you contradict yourself or change course without a good reason, the girls will be sure to notice and you will be in for problems.

Tip: To feel appreciated is the deepest human need.

Chapter 14

Anything You Can Do,
I Can Do Better

Vanessa:

Recently a coach asked me whether it's better to have the most talented players out there, or those who play the best together. Simply put: What's better to have, chemistry or talent? It is a really good question. Herb Brooks, coach of the 1980 gold medal U.S. Olympic hockey team, said, "I'm not looking for the BEST players. I'm looking for the RIGHT players."

Our team just went through a season where we played our most talented players, with little thought of chemistry. Now and then it was impressive to watch. Other times, we failed miserably. Girls screamed at each other during the game or by the water cooler when it was over.

How would you act if your boss told you what an awful job you did on this assignment? What if your boss said you have no future in the company, and that a monkey could do the job you're doing? Would you work harder? Or feel so down that you started doing even less?

Everyone is different, but typically if someone gets the message they don't have a shot at something and everyone around them does, they don't work harder. They don't continue to love the job or the sport. They do it like it's a chore and they don't care when it starts or when it ends.

And that's the chemistry versus talent debate. If I make a mistake and my co-worker or teammate tells me I stink at what I do, or doesn't say anything at all, or rolls her eyes, or doesn't slap my hand, I am feeling pretty crappy.

Now we're in a game together, and there's no trust. This lack of trust leads to a blown play. That needs to happen only one time, and all of a sudden it's a domino effect. Other mistakes start happening because the trust and communication break down. The chemistry dissolves. And just like that, the other team has the momentum. Even with talented players, a team might not be able to get out of that situation.

Team bonding can be a fun time to grow and learn more about each other. We've had pasta dinners, scavenger hunts, movie nights. But there always seems to be at least one girl who has a problem with what we're doing. She complains about the time, the day, or the activity. Sometimes she says she has homework. I always wondered what the issue was. At college when I would host pasta dinners, most players would be out the door before I even finished cleaning up their dinner plates.

It wasn't that way in high school. We had pasta dinners before every big game. We would stay until we got kicked out! I always thought the two were related. If a team wants to be together outside the gym and can enjoy, or at least tolerate, each other's company, the team will soon learn to be just that: a team. Players will grow together, challenge each other, enjoy playing together and in the end, build chemistry. The teams that can't sit together for more than 30 minutes, the teams that can't have all members at a team dinner or movie night, those are the teams that are in extreme trouble.

Amy was coach's prize pupil. The golden child. She could do no wrong in his eyes. He truly believed we could never win without her. She was one of those players who was never OK to practice, but always felt perfect on game day. She never had to follow any type of team rule. For everyone else, you couldn't start if you didn't practice. Not Amy. She always stayed on the court. Once she felt sore and tired, so she didn't play. Her sub went in and was playing pretty well. Then she made one mistake, and the coach pulled her out right away. Amy went back in and made four mistakes in a row. No one ever got as many chances as Amy did. She was definitely the go-to player on the team. Her priorities were breaking records and having the best statistics. That's not my opinion. Amy actually wrote that on the paper she turned in.

Having an Amy on the team was more of a negative influence than any other team issue I've seen. Girls were beside themselves trying to wrap their head around her selfish attitude and trying to understand why they had to sit out a game for missing practice when she didn't. Even more than that, Amy was a smart talker. She knew exactly whom she had to manipulate to get everything she wanted. Assistant coaches saw right through Amy, and that's why she never had a good relationship with them. But the head coach, the person who truly mattered, saw what he wanted to see. He believed you play the most talented players even if they all hate each other, because when they start winning they'll learn to love each other. They'll put the team first when success comes their way. Maybe. Maybe not.

Wherever there's an Amy, there's a Kelly. She wants to know why the coach favors Amy. What do you say to Kelly? Try to hang in there because you'll maybe get a chance if Amy gets hurt?

Meanwhile, the head coach wants to know why Kelly is being so selfish. She's not being selfish. She's frustrated and confused and she wants answers, even if the answer is Amy is the better player right now.

There needs to be some line of communication. Honest communication.

Double standards are a chemistry-killer. It's unfair if half the team must show up on time, while the other few girls don't have to. It's unfair to hold the team accountable for grades, then overlook some who are failing classes. When your players start seeing favoritism, they'll start being defiant. It's a guarantee. They'll lose trust in you as a coach, teammates will start bickering, and tensions will rise. More harm will come from making one player the star of your team than any good that will come out of it.

I would love to re-create a "Remember the Titans" team. Have you seen the movie? It's about a newly integrated team that comes together when the community around them is having trouble doing so. In my mind I bring different players and people together and challenge them to become family despite all their differences. I wish that in the games like the championship, I could say, "You are doing all you can, and that's good enough." And my captain would stand up and say, "No, Coach, it's not. You demanded perfection and that's what we need," and they would all come together despite the issues and win together and celebrate together and love each other and put all the crap to the side.

It's hard to do.

Tip: Double standards are a killer.

Chapter 15

Santa, Goose Poop, and Film

From Mike:

Years ago I was a running a summer sports camp at a small girls school. There was no air-conditioning, and the heat index had climbed well into the 90s. Halfway through the week, aiming to break the routine, I wore a Santa Claus cap. You know, Christmas in July?

It did not go well. As you can imagine, the girls wanted to know why I was wearing a Santa cap. Even when I explained it, they didn't seem to like it the way I was hoping they would. They thought it was strange, period.

Fast forward a bit. Now I'm helping out with the lacrosse team, a very young program. We go on the road, and when we get to the host school, our girls are grossed out. A gaggle of geese lived on or near the field, and had left droppings to prove it. Our players could think of nothing else. After listening to the comments and expressions of disgust, we called in the girls and said, "Listen. There's goose poop on the field. There's nothing we can do about it. Let's go out and play our game."

Back then our game wasn't very good, so we lost. To this day I think of that game as a horror movie: "The Day of the Goose Poop."

Looking back on things, I wonder if perhaps the Santa hat and the goose poop have more in common than you might think. In both cases, something distracted the athletes. In both cases, the athletes found it hard to get past it.

This all comes to mind when the topic of watching film comes up. As a coach you might think it's a brilliant idea, and maybe it is. Watching film can add another dimension to your coaching. It gives visual feedback when verbal cues are not working. But as with so many other aspects of coaching girls, you've got to know some things before you begin, or else you might be introducing a distraction, and your athletes will find it hard to get past it.

Vanessa:

I've heard coaches complain that their players don't take film study seriously.

That depends.

If you don't make something a consistent part of your routine, people in general don't seem to understand the reason for the sudden change. When you watch film only now and then, the girls won't stop commenting on how they look, and what their last play just looked like, and what a silly motion their bodies just made.

"We can stop if you guys aren't going to take this seriously" is what comes out of the coach's mouth.

Girls need time to adjust to watching themselves on film. At first they are excited, and their attention is flying all over the screen. It will get better. Give them an opportunity to accept what they look like then guide their eyes and attention to what you want them to be watching.

It is really helpful to give them something to focus on. "When the other team is doing THIS, I want us to be doing THAT." Giving them specific areas of focus will invite conversation, attention, and mindful learning. Without this guidance, watching film will be just another thing your players cannot get past. I recently worked with a head coach who gave our players this guidance. He asked the girls to focus on specific techniques. He did a great job focusing the attention and demanding the mindful learning previously mentioned.

Unfortunately, too often film watching is not delivered with this guidance. Coaches throw players into a room. They want the players to see the good and the bad and then form an opinion. There is too much going on for that to be productive. And when it's not productive, coaches seem to get frustrated and think to themselves, "This is why we don't watch film. Let's get back into the gym."

There's a story told of film sessions with legendary football coach Vince Lombardi. His comments would be so sharp that even grown men -- some of the toughest people anywhere -- would have their egos reduced to rubble. One player, so afraid of Lombardi's scorn, would stand up and criticize himself before the coach could. "Look at that," he'd point to his mistake on the screen. "That's disgusting. I should know better. I let you all down with that play."

If watching film could make NFL football players quake in fear, imagine what effect it could have on young girls.

Make sure that your film watching isn't random; let's say on a rainy day or when you haven't had time to prepare practice. Give the girls at least one session to get used to it. Be constructive. Praise the positive when you see it. And try not to embarrass anyone by singling out one player in front of the whole team.

Tip: Value routines, and don't break them without a good reason.

"Women speak two languages — one of which is verbal."

-- Shakespeare

Chapter 16

Who Are Your Players?

Mike:

Maybe you've heard this story. It takes place in a nursing school, where one day the professor gives a pop quiz. All the questions seem normal enough, except the last one: "What is the first name of the woman who cleans the school?"

Taken by surprise, the students ask the professor if that question counts toward their grade. There they get a lesson in real nursing: "In your careers," the professor said, "you will meet many people. All are significant. They deserve your attention and care."

Coaches can learn that lesson as well. Players are more than chess pieces who wander in and out of your life on certain days of the week. They are people with lives, hopes and interests of their own.

Vanessa:

I'm not saying you should never be tough on your players. Instead, I'm asking you to challenge yourself as a coach. Have you made the effort to truly know your players? Have you demanded something from them and shown appreciation when they've met your expectations? If they haven't met your expectations yet, are they still doing everything they possibly can? If so, do they know you're proud of them? As coaches we always preach being one team. Are you a part of that team? Or is it all of them together, and then you?

How well do you know your players? If you've spent more than one season with them and still don't know what makes them respond, chances are you're not taking the necessary time to find out. You might discover that knowing your player as a person is a great investment of your time and energy.

Tip: Learn what makes your team respond best.

Chapter 17

Drama Class

Vanessa:

One day I watched a sport psychologist work with a team. He wanted everyone to be on the same page. Same goals, same work ethic, same dedication. As part of a team-building exercise, he handed out index cards. Then he asked every player to write three things about each teammate: two positive things and one thing to work on.

The girls read them and felt inspired to work on their weaknesses and appreciate their strengths. Reading 30 positives made them feel happy.

This technique worked so well I decided to use it with one of my teams, a team with lots of issues. After the index cards came back and the players read their cards, I had about seven girls in tears. All at the same time. I really started panicking. What is wrong?

"All 15 people think I need to work on my serving," said one.

OK, look at it like that's the only weakness you have! That's good!

"NO! ALL 15 PEOPLE THINK I CAN'T SERVE," she said, running out of the gym.

Another other girl, crying, said, "And I have 15 different weaknesses. So basically I suck at everything!"

She ran out, too.

Oh boy, did that team activity backfire. I didn't try that one for the next couple of years.

From Mike:

As I cut and paste Vanessa's words, I start to laugh. Not because I think crying is funny, but because I've been there. Sometimes the more you try, the more things blow up. It reminds me of playing softball in the New York Press League. One day my team was playing against our archrival. They hammered us, and that wasn't even the worst thing. The worst thing was that EVERYTHING they hit turned into gold. Long hits, short hits, everything in between. Finally, one of their batters hit a weak popup that should have been an out. Instead it looped over the infield and fell for what must have been their 30th hit of the day. I just started to laugh. My teammates must have thought I was crazy. What's so funny about getting your butt kicked? But the absurdity of it just got to me. Here's Vanessa with the story of another team-building effort gone horribly wrong.

Vanessa:

One night our team-bonding trip was to go to Wawa for these delicious milkshakes they love so much. Three girls ran upstairs to their rooms and asked the girls driving to wait until they came back. But when they returned, the cars were all gone. Those three girls didn't get the chance to go out with the team that night.

When I told the male coaches what happened at what was supposed to be a mandatory team bonding, they shrugged it off. "Oh well," they seemed to be saying. "What are you going to do?" Theses coaches didn't get it. I knew this episode meant a lot more than just an "oh well." In a girl's world, this just started extreme drama and even more tension at practice.

One year we started keeping journals. After every session athletes would write their impressions, then turn them in. We originally asked the players to write notes from practice: what we talked about, what they learned, what we watched during film. It didn't turn that way; it wound up being about emotions and feelings, and problems with players, with drills, and with the energy of practice. After games we learned how differently girls saw things. One would say, "We finally played as team out there today!" while another would write, "I felt like I had absolutely no one's support." There were many positives in reading the journals every week, and some negatives as well. Overall, I think it helped us learn who our players are. It helped us understand what they got out of certain meetings, games, and drills. There were a couple of times when a meeting would end and the coaches would say, "Wow, that went well." Then we would read a journal and learn the girl went back to her room and cried. When we asked her why she was so upset, we found she thought the meeting went badly.

Sometimes you can't win.

Tip: Keep trying.

Chapter 18

Your Biggest Challenge

Vanessa:

Earlier I mentioned I would love to re-create "Remember the Titans." Well, I might not be able to re-create the exact movie and have it pan out that way, but now I try to do everything with one purpose. And that purpose is to get everyone on the same page so when the going gets tough, my team gets going. I make note of the girls who are playing well with each other, and I really try to work with the ones who aren't. I believe in constant mixing and matching when it comes to scrimmages and team drills, so everyone is comfortable playing with everyone.

Creating a team by writing names on a piece of paper is the easy part. Pushing through those personalities, weaknesses and skills, to ultimately become a family is a challenge. And if you're a coach, you're telling everyone you've accepted this challenge.

Building the team's morale and confidence is what brings players together. Another team or program is going to come into your gym, your field, your court, and try to knock your team down. When this happens, your players have to know that you believe in them and support them. They must all have each other's backs. That comes with constant praise, appreciation and positive feedback. No girl should have the "my coach just hates me" mentality. If she does, you can give all the feedback you want, and it won't matter. No one will apply it, because all your athletes will hear is, "You stink."

You wouldn't let any outsider come in and bully your family, so why should you be allowed to? Believe in your players.

Tip: Work constantly to get girls on the same page.

Chapter 19

Tougher Than You Think

Vanessa:

When men discuss females, they say things like:

"They are SO sensitive!"

"They cry over everything!"

"We need to figure out females."

"How do we speak to them without them breaking down and taking everything personally?"

"Females are just impossible."

"Can't live with them, can't live without them."

True, girls are sensitive. They do cry, and they do take things personally. I believe men react to this by believing they must sugarcoat what they say so there are no crazy breakdowns. Wrong.

Just because we can be sensitive and take things personally doesn't mean that we can't always handle the truth.

My coach in high school proved it. She was the first person to let us know when we weren't doing something right. She set high standards and would be very blunt when we didn't meet them.

In my freshman year, our team won the league title, the state title, and Tournament of Champions. We were the best team in the state! To this day it remains the best, most amazing sports experience ever. But (yes, there is a but) I always just wanted to make my coaches proud, my team proud. That was the constant payoff. I would beat myself up if

I played poorly or made mistakes that would hurt the team. I put so much pressure on myself that I invariably would play worse.

My coach was so in tune with her players that she quickly saw my game behavior and made me change it. I started taking the pressure off myself and just started having fun with the sport I loved. Over the four years of high school, I became the most mentally strong athlete I could imagine, and I owe it all to her. We were taught to be mentally stronger than external factors like bad calls, timeouts, large crowds and game-point. It was my best learning experience ever, because it changed me as a person throughout all aspects of my life. I became a better student, a better friend and a better worker. My determination and hustle made me proactive in my college search, job search, and any other project, including this book.

Look carefully at what happened. Our coach didn't sugarcoat things. She didn't coddle. She said what needed to be said. At the same time, she was in tune with us. That mixture created championship players and championship people.

Tip: Girls are different, not weaker.

Chapter 20

Rethink the Puzzle

Mike:

Little things about coaching girls used to drive me crazy. Take the warm-up. I'd say, "Get a partner and start throwing and catching." Then I'd wait, steaming, as they just stood around. "Why are there no balls in the air," I would demand, watching precious practice time disappear. Turns out the girls weren't just standing around. They were doing what they are wired to do. Girls create networks. They must pay attention to the network, making sure it is strong, that the right people are included, and that no one is excluded. So the simple act of trying to select a partner for the drill would put their brain circuits into overdrive.

Another behavior that would push my buttons was the socializing before a game or practice. I used to fume while girls chatted. Why didn't they get right to work? Again, what I thought was aimless activity was anything but. Girls need time to connect, even if they've been in school together all day long.

In both cases, I've learned to live with the delay. Wasting gym time always bothers me, but it's not a waste of time when girls check out their networks.

Years of coaching, with input from Vanessa and other women with whom I've worked, have taught me some patience. Not a lot, but a little bit. When I see something I don't like or don't understand, I can step back and remember what's true: Girls are different.

Tip: Get fascinated by, and not frustrated with, the female psyche.

Chapter 21

Our Post-Season Talk

From Vanessa:

At the end of a sports season, any good coaching staff will take time to reflect: What went wrong? What went right? Where we can improve? One year the conversation was specific to females, their emotions, and how coaching is more than just teaching sports. When we got into how we could improve the next season, my response was along the lines of "We can teach techniques all we want, but if the players are not a team, they're not responding well to us, and they're not mentally strong enough to compete at high levels, then we have more to worry about than technique." Some men will agree and try to adjust. Others will ignore the advice and go on coaching as before. They think that excelling at a sport is nothing more than practice, strategy and watching film.

And it makes me want to ask them, "Do you know *any* females?"

From Mike:

I'm grateful to Vanessa and others who are educating me on coaching girls. I wince when I think of all the times I neglected -- or was not even aware of -- the social and emotional aspect of my players. This neglect no doubt cost us some games. But just as we hope our athletes develop, we as coaches must do the same.

As the result of writing this book, I'm adding a category to my daily practice plans. It will be called simply "Girls," and will force me to think more deeply about chemistry and communication.

Actually, this idea is borrowed from Bobby Hurley, legendary basketball coach at St. Anthony High School in Jersey City, NJ. Coach Hurley follows a "20-minute rule" in his practices: He makes it a point to give each player on his team a compliment in the first 20 minutes of practice.

It's harder than it sounds. Knowing that you must give a compliment forces you to pay attention. It forces you to notice what's right. This gives you a chance to notice which player needs a pat on the back, which one could use some one-on-one communication, or which one is caught in some unproductive dynamic.

In sum, committing to touch base with every player on the team every single day will make you more aware, more open, more in tune with the team.

Remember what Vanessa said in an earlier chapter? The very best year of her athletic career came under a coach who demanded a lot while at the same time staying in tune with the players.

It sounds like a great way for all of us to move forward.

Tip: Committing to give compliments forces you to notice what is right.

Chapter 22

Final Note from Mike

In writing this book and reflecting on a quarter-century of coaching, I can't help but love comedian George Carlin's take on men and women.

"Here's all you have to know about men and women: Women are crazy, men are stupid. And the main reason women are crazy is that men are stupid."

Hey, it's not my fault. I was born that way. But it is my fault if I don't try to learn and to change.

That's what I'm trying to.

Years too late, when I first began coaching at a tiny Catholic all-girls school, we would return from a game in which we were outclassed.

"How did you do," the principal would ask.

"We lost 22-0," I would reply.

"Well," she persisted. "Did you have fun?"

Umm, no. We lost 22-0. There's nothing fun about that.

Back then I believed it was my job to change a culture in which getting stomped could even remotely be viewed as fun. And to a certain extent I did.

What I didn't realize until now is that the principal's question was designed to change my culture as well. I had to stop thinking about everything in terms of outcomes and start thinking about process.

Now I understand a bit better. Some of that understanding has come from working with female coaches. Some of it has come from writing this with Vanessa.

Either way, there's a saying that when the pupil is ready, the teacher will appear.

Better late than never.

So to any of my former players out there, especially those who did not have enough fun on my team, I apologize. To those who've been kind enough to say that somehow I've made a difference, thank you.

If you're wondering what qualifies me to write a book about coaching girls, here's the answer:

Nothing qualifies me. I'm just trying to help coaches avoid the mistakes I've made.

After all, as physicist Neils Bohr said, "An expert is someone who has made all the mistakes which can be made in a narrow field."

Yup.

Chapter 23

Final Note from Vanessa

I have interviewed more 60 females, hearing their stories and creating new friendships along the way. I have spoken with them about several topics related to sports and writing this book, but there's one thing I asked them to answer after every interview was over. What would you say to a younger you? What advice would you give to yourself, or other young female athletes, as they embark on their athletic journey? So here's mine:

If you are a female athlete reading this book, I want to encourage you to have a voice. Demand respect and appreciation from those around you! Always feel strong and confident enough to ask questions, and always, always, ALWAYS stand up for yourself.

My mother continually told me, "You are your own best advocate. No one will fight for you if you don't fight for yourself!"

Nothing in this lifetime will be handed to you, so be ready to put in the hard work. It won't be easy. It won't be easy. It won't be easy. You will come across amazing coaches, and you will come across terrible ones; you need to be equally respectful regardless. Never settle for average: Average is just as close to the bottom as it is to the top.

Train hard and sweat when no one is watching because that's where your character will be built. Don't ever allow someone else to make you fall out of love with a sport. If you choose to move on, that's fine. But make sure it's your choice and only your choice. Celebrate the joys of winning and succeeding, but train every day as if you're in last place.

Sometimes, no matter how hard you work or how well you think you are performing you might not get the opportunity you think you deserve. Be patient and keep working hard. Learn to be a supportive teammate on the bench as well as when you're in the game. Be a part of a program or organization that is bigger than just yourself, and accept and embrace that. Push the girls around you, push yourself. Leave your comfort zone.

Mia Hamm said it best, "I learned a long time ago that there is something worse than missing the goal, and that's not pulling the trigger."

If you can dream it, you can achieve it.

Tell me YOUR story here:

Vanessa-Sullivan@hotmail.com

Appendix I

Suggested Reading

Training Soccer Champions. By Anson Dorrance

Men Are from Mars, Women Are from Venus. By John Gray

Catch Them Being Good: Everything You Need to Know to Successfully Coach Girls. By Tony DiCicco and Colleen Hacker.

The Female Brain. By Louann Brizendine

Women Who Win: Female Athletes on Being the Best. By Lisa Taggart

InSideOut Coaching: How Sports Can Transform Lives. By Joe Ehrmann

Gender and Competition: How Men and Women Approach Work and Play Differently. By Kathleen DeBoer

Top Dog: The Science of Winning and Losing. By Ashley Merriman and Po Bronson

Raising Our Athletic Daughters: How Sports Can Build Self-Esteem And Save Girls' Lives. By Jean Zimmerman

In These Girls, Hope Is a Muscle. By Madeleine Blais

Go for the Goal! A Champion's Guide to Winning in Soccer and Life. By Mia Hamm

Odd Girl Out: The Hidden Culture of Aggression in Girls. By Rachel Simmons

Brave Girl Eating: A Family's Struggle with Anorexia. By Harriet Brown

Bossypants. By Tina Fay

Go Girl: An Inspiring Journey from Bronze to Gold. By Natalie Cook

Why She Buys: The New Strategy for Reaching the World's Most Powerful Consumers. By Bridget Brennan

Appendix II

A Peek into Players' Brains (And Hearts)

During one of her coaching seasons, Vanessa used a brilliant strategy to get to know her players and to inspire them. She asked each one to write a favorite quote. Then she compiled a list, made copies and placed them all around the locker room.

This strategy works in multiple ways:

1. It gives the coach insight into what the athlete is thinking and what issues may be going on.
2. It makes the player go public. By writing something, she owns it.
3. It provides a coaching point for the future. If a player is having a bad day, the coach can challenge her to live up to what she has written.

You can use variations of this theme. Vanessa recalls that one of her coaches invited each player to identify and write down what she wanted to leave behind: frustration, selfishness, doubt, fear.

You can also challenge them to write their goals.

Here are the actual quotes submitted by members of Vanessa's team:

"Hard work does not necessarily guarantee success, but no success is possible without hard work."

"Never set limits, chase after your dreams, and don't be afraid to go out of your comfort zone, and do so by having a laugh and a positive heart."

"The difference between a successful person and others is not a lack of strength, not a lack of knowledge, but rather a lack of will."

"Let it go."

"Treat people with all of the love and respect that you want to be treated with, and don't allow anyone to treat you with less love and respect than you are willing to give them."

"Follow your dreams, have faith, stay strong, make your own path, and enjoy every minute. Life is what you make of it. Live, laugh, love, and don't forget to dance!"

"It all works out."

"What do you want? Go out and get it."

"Go kill it, kid."

"Everything always works out in the long run and will be okay."

"Character is both developed and revealed by the tests of life."

"Great challenges make life interesting; overcoming them makes life meaningful. It's how you deal with failure that determines your happiness and success."

"Don't let anybody tell you can't, because you can do anything!"

"Don't ever doubt yourself... or what you're capable of."

"Your mind will quit before your body does."

"In order to succeed, your desire for success should be greater than your fear of failure."

"Save the drama for your mama!"

"Anyone can support a team that is winning – it takes no courage. But to stand behind a team, to defend a team when they are down and really need you, that takes a lot of courage."

"Train your mind to fully believe mediocrity is not acceptable. GOOD isn't good enough! Strive for great, excellent, superb."

"You don't get over it – you get through it. You don't move on – you move forward. Don't ever settle for average. Average is just as close to the bottom as it is to the top."

"You may encounter many defeats, but you must not be defeated. In fact, it may be necessary to encounter the defeats, so you can know who you are, what you can rise from, and how you can still come out of it."

Appendix III

Quotes by and About Women Athletes

"I just try to concentrate on concentrating." -- *Martina Navratilova, tennis legend*

"Believe me, the reward is not so great without the struggle." -- *Wilma Rudolph, Olympic track champion*

"True champions aren't always the ones that win, but those with the most guts." -- *Mia Hamm, soccer superstar*

"I prefer to train in the dark, cold winter months when it takes a stern attitude to get out of bed before dawn and head out the door to below-freezing weather conditions. Anyone can run on a nice, warm, brisk day." -- *Grete Waitz, renowned marathoner*

"All of my life I have always had the urge to do things better than anybody else." -- *Babe Didrikson Zaharias, American star in golf, basketball and track and field*

"Susie had no talent whatsoever. She's a little person who couldn't even make a final at a state meet - coming and showing the world that on sheer guts and determination you can do anything you want!" -- *Susie Maroney's coach, Dick Caine, after her marathon swim from Mexico to Cuba*

"I think sports gave me the first place where this awkward girl could feel comfortable in my own skin. I think that's true for a lot of women—sports gives you a part of your life where you can work at something and you look in the mirror and you like that person." -- *Teri McKeever, first woman to serve as head coach of a U.S. Olympic swimming team.*

"I don't run away from a challenge because I am afraid. Instead, I run toward it because the only way to escape fear is to trample it beneath your feet." -- *Nadia Comaneci, first female gymnast to receive a perfect 10 in Olympic competition.*

"When I was 12, I had a coach tell me I would never be a championship pitcher. That devastated me. I was crushed." -- *Jennie Finch, Olympic gold medalist in 2004.*

Thank you for taking your valuable time to read this. We wish you continued success in sports and in life.

All the best,
Vanessa Sullivan and Mike Tully

89668313R00071

Made in the USA
Lexington, KY
02 June 2018